Copyright © 2020 by Eric Goldinger

DISCLAIMER

By reading this disclaimer, you fully accept the terms of this disclaimer. If you are not in agreement with this disclaimer, please do not order or read this book. The content of this book is provided for information and educational purposes only.

Table of Contents

INTRODUCTION

Consider setting up a patio vegetable garden if you are looking for a way to grow vegetables and fruits, which does not entail half an acre of land and a strong back. All you need to start growing today is a sunny place, some pots, potting soil, and the right veggies on a relatively level surface. I 'm going to guide you through the process of setting up and maintaining your own patio vegetable garden in this book.

Time, effort, money and maintenance are needed for a beautiful garden. Starting with a good plan for the garden will help to will all of those things. Before getting to work, thinking about your yard or garden will create a cohesive area that accentuates your home and provides years of enjoyment.

The two practices associated with the cultivation of plants are gardening and horticulture.

Although there is a great deal of overlap between the two practices, the former refers to a recreational activity performed by home or hobbyist gardeners, while the latter refers to a skilled career that is scientifically validated and highly specialized. There are major variations in the methods, technologies and scales of operation, despite the undoubted similarities. Different methods of cultivation, such as organic gardening, are used to illustrate the variations in the approach between gardening and horticulture, while garden styles or activities such as patio gardening or allotment gardening are used to show that while gardeners are buyers of products and services, professional horticulturalists are not only suppliers of products and services, they also have allotments. Commercial cultivation and botanical gardens are studied as horticultural practices, thus acknowledging that, in the strict use of the term, some of the most professional growers are amateurs and specialist societies tend to them. Differences in approach and size are discussed in techniques such as soil cultivation, propagation and pruning, and the chapter ends with examples of the variety of research efforts underpinning plant breeding, construction of glasshouses, and media for cultivation.

Why Grow a Patio Garden?

Making the most of the small space you have is as simple as combining a few clever gardening techniques and strategies to meet your expectations. Your patio garden plan might include the use of vertical gardening, raised bed gardening, and container gardening. Each of these techniques is a successful way to garden in confined or small areas. But why bother going through the effort to create a patio garden in the first place?

There are so many wonderful benefit that you can derive from the simple planning of a patio garden. It really only makes sense to do so.

Patio Gardens Create Extra Living Space

One of the experiences that you might be going through is that you have outgrown your home, apartment, or condo. Although it seems as though you are going to have plenty of space when you move in, quite often, you outgrow that interior space rather quickly. Designing an outdoor patio garden is a simple yet effective strategy for extending your living space to the outdoors.

How you decide to use that outside space is up to you, but however that is, you gain extra living space that you wouldn't otherwise have. When designing your patio garden, you should keep in mind your primary purpose (beside the fact that you want and need more room to enjoy life) and design your garden around that focal point. One of the options you have is to create a multi-purpose space where you can sit down and relax while enjoying a good book, sit at a table and enjoy a meal garnished with freshly-grown herbs, and entertain family and friends with a short stroll around your private garden.

Patio Gardens Hide Eyesores

Just because you have a patio, it does not mean that you have an attractive one or a gorgeous view. Creating a patio garden can be a perfect strategy for improving your view by hiding eyesores behind attractive plants and planters. You can use a variety of ground-level planters to hide imperfections in the patio floor while using vertical gardening techniques to hide unsightly places higher up.

Patio Gardens Create Relaxing Environments

Designing a patio garden for a relaxing environment to unwind in is one of the best reasons for doing so. All too often, people today spend their days running from one task to the next without even having time to take a breather so they can sit down and relax.

However, when you design your patio as a secret getaway, a sort of private sanctuary, then you have good reason to simply sit and relax without worrying about the list of unfinished errands or tomorrow's to-do list.

In addition to your plants, you might want to consider adding a small fountain or attractive wind chimes. The can add to the relaxing aura of your garden sanctuary. The dulcet sounds emitted from either of these will add to the beauty of your plants and the décor of your patio garden.

Patios Create Spaces to Garden

Gardening can be a relaxing hobby that gets you out into the sunshine for a chance at some fresh air. Even in the city, it is nice to go outdoors and feel the warmth of the sun's rays on your face while breathing in nearby scents. Just imagine how nice it will be to breathe in the freshness of your personal garden plants!

The patio can be used to create a convenient space for a garden when you have a small yard or live in an apartment or condo. It is convenient because it is typically right outside one of your doors. For those of you who live in the city but enjoy the outdoors, a patio can give you the chance to create your own little getaway filled with colorful plants, decorative containers, and the scents that only Mother Nature can provide.

When you garden, you can enjoy the company of friends and family or you can do it on your own. Either way, you can enjoy a few relaxing moments each day along with the satisfaction that comes from watching plants grow. Patio gardens are great for growing herbs, flowers, vegetables, and fruits. If you are new to gardening, you might want to start out on a small scale by selecting just a few varieties of plants and seeing how well you do. Simply create a garden plan, select your plants, and get started. You can focus on one specific type of gardening or incorporate several styles.

In addition to your plants, you might want to consider adding a small fountain or attractive wind chimes. The can add to the relaxing aura of your garden sanctuary. The dulcet sounds emitted from either of these will add to the beauty of your plants and the décor of your patio garden.

Patio Gardens are Places to Entertain

A patio garden provides an attractive place to entertain guests. Whether you are into relaxing in an outdoor hot tub or enjoy grilling up a tasty barbecue dinner, the patio garden is the perfect scenario. The style of furniture you purchase depends on the type of entertaining that you intend to do.

If you choose barbecuing, then your focus is going to be on a table, chairs, and a grill. The plants that you include in your garden might include common vegetables found at many outdoor barbecue functions. This can include peppers, tomatoes, cucumbers, lettuce, and a pleasant variety of herbs.

If you prefer to do your entertaining from the comfort of a hot tub, then your garden might have a bit more focus on plants that can act as a bit of a deterrent to insects due to their scent. This typically includes a variety of pungent herbs and flowers.

One of the nicest facets to outdoor entertaining is the focus on lush foliage that is attractive and soothing. From the bright colors of the plants to the fresh scents emanating from them, your guests can enjoy a taste of the beautiful outdoors in a relaxed setting.

GARDENING

Gardening is the art of growing plants. Garden cultivation allows ornamental plants grown normally for their flowers, foliage, overall appearance, or for their dyes. Useful plants are grown for consumption (vegetables, fruits, herbs, and leaf vegetables) or for medicinal use. A gardener is someone who practices gardening.

Gardening ranges in scale from fruit orchards, to long boulevard plantings with one or more different types of shrubs, trees and herbaceous plants, to residential yards including lawns and foundation plantings, to large or small containers grown inside or outside.

Gardening can be very specialized, with only one type of plant grown, or may include a large number of different plants in mixed plantings. It requires active involvement in plant breeding and appears to be labour-intensive, which separates it from agriculture or forestry.

Gardening for food dates back to prehistory. Ornamental gardens were known in ancient times, and the Hanging Gardens of Babylon were a famous example, while ancient Rome had hundreds of gardens.

Types of Gardens

The domestic garden can assume almost any identity the owner wishes within the limits of climate, materials, and means. The size of the plot is one of the main factors, deciding not only the scope but also the kind of display and usage. Limits on space near urban centres, as well as the wish to spend less time on upkeep, have tended to make modern gardens ever smaller. Paradoxically, this happens at a time when the variety of plants and hybrids has never been wider. The wise small gardener avoids the temptations of this banquet. Some of the most attractive miniature schemes, such as those seen in Japan or in some Western patio gardens, are effectively based on an austere simplicity of design and content, with a handful of plants given room to find their proper identities.

In the medium- to large-sized garden, the tradition generally continues of dividing the area to serve various purposes: a main ornamental section to enhance the residence and provide vistas; walkways and seating areas for recreation; a vegetable plot; a children's play area; and features to catch the eye here and there. Because most gardens are mixed, the resulting style is a matter of emphasis rather than exclusive concentration on one aspect. It may be useful to review briefly the main garden types.

Flower Gardens

Though flower gardens in different countries may vary in the types of plants that are grown, the basic planning and principles are nearly the same, whether the gardens are formal or informal. Trees and shrubs are the mainstay of a well-designed flower garden. These permanent features are usually planned first, and the spaces for herbaceous plants, annuals, and bulbs are arranged around them. The range of flowering trees and shrubs is enormous. It is important, however, that such plants be appropriate to the areas they will occupy when mature. Thus it is of little use to plant a forest tree that will grow 100 feet (30 metres) high and 50 feet across in a small suburban front garden 30 feet square, but a narrow flowering cherry or redbud tree would be quite suitable.

Blending and contrast of colour as well as of forms are important aspects to consider in planning a garden. The older type of herbaceous border was designed to give a maximum display of colour in summer, but many gardeners now prefer to have flowers during the early spring as well, at the expense of some bare patches later. This is often done by planting early-flowering bulbs in groups toward the front. Mixed borders of flowering shrubs combined with herbaceous plants are also popular and do not require quite so much maintenance as the completely herbaceous border.

Groups of half-hardy annuals, which can withstand low night temperatures, may be planted at the end of spring to fill gaps left by the spring-flowering bulbs. The perpetual-flowering roses and some of the larger shrub roses look good toward the back of such a border, but the hybrid tea roses and the floribunda and polyantha roses are usually grown in separate rose beds or in a rose garden by themselves.

Woodland Gardens

The informal woodland garden is the natural descendant of the shrubby "wilderness" of earlier times. The essence of the woodland garden is informality and naturalness. Paths curve rather than run straight and are of mulch or grass rather than pavement. Trees are thinned to allow enough light, particularly in the glades, but irregular groups may be left, and any mature tree of character can be a focal point. Plants are chosen largely from those that are woodlanders in their native countries: rhododendron, magnolia, pieris, and maple among the trees and shrubs; lily, daffodil, and snowdrop among the bulbs; primrose, hellebore, St.-John's-wort, epimedium, and many others among the herbs.

Rock Gardens

Rock gardens are designed to look as if they are a natural part of a rocky hillside or slope. If rocks are added, they are generally laid on their larger edges, as in natural strata. A few large boulders usually look better than a number of small rocks. In a well-designed rock garden, rocks are arranged so that there are various exposures for sun-tolerant plants such as rockroses and for shade-tolerant plants such as primulas, which often do better in a cool, north-facing aspect. Many smaller perennial plants are available for filling spaces in vertical cracks among the rock faces.

The main rocks from which rock gardens are constructed are sandstone and limestone. Sandstone, less irregular and pitted generally, looks more restful and natural, but certain plants, notably most of the dianthuses, do best in limestone. Granite is generally regarded as too hard and unsuitable for the rock garden because it weathers very slowly.

Water Gardens

The water garden represents one of the oldest forms of gardening. Egyptian records and pictures of cultivated water lilies date as far back as 2000 bce. The Japanese have also made water gardens to their own particular and beautiful patterns for many centuries. Many have an ornamental lantern of stone in the centre or perhaps a flat trellis roof of wisteria extending over the water. In Europe and North America, water gardens range from formal pools with rectangular or circular outline, sometimes with fountains in the centre and often without plants or with just one or two water lilies (Nymphaea), to informal pools of irregular outline planted with water lilies and other water plants and surrounded by boggy or damp soil where moisture-tolerant plants can be grown. The pool must contain suitable oxygenating plants to keep the water clear and support any introduced fish. Most water plants, including even the large water lilies, do well in still water two to five feet deep. Temperate water lilies flower all day, but many of the tropical and subtropical ones open their flowers only in the evening.

In temperate countries water gardens also can be made under glass, and the pools can be kept heated. In such cases, more tropical plants, such as the great Victoria amazonica (V. regia) or the lotus (Nelumbo nucifera), can be grown together with papyrus reeds at the edge. The range of moisture-loving plants for damp places at the edge of the pool is great and includes many beautiful plants such as the candelabra primulas, calthas, irises, and osmunda ferns.

Herb and Vegetable Gardens

Most of the medieval gardens and the first botanical gardens were largely herb gardens containing plants used for medicinal purposes or herbs such as thyme, parsley, rosemary, fennel, marjoram, and dill for savouring foods. The term herb garden is usually used now to denote a garden of herbs used for cooking, and the medicinal aspect is rarely considered. Herb gardens need a sunny position, because the majority of the plants grown are native to warm, dry regions.

The vegetable garden also requires an open and sunny location. Good cultivation and preparation of the ground are important for successful vegetable growing, and it is also desirable to practice a rotation of crops as in farming. The usual period of rotation for vegetables is three years; this also helps to prevent the carryover from season to season of certain pests and diseases.

The old French potager, the prized vegetable garden, was grown to be decorative as well as useful; the short rows with little hedges around and the high standard of cultivation represent a model of the art of vegetable growing. The elaborate parterre vegetable garden at the Château de Villandry is perhaps the finest example in Europe of a decorative vegetable garden.

Specialty Gardens

Roof Gardens

The modern tendency in architecture for flat roofs has made possible the development of attractive roof gardens in urban areas above private houses and commercial buildings. These gardens follow the same principles as others except that the depth of soil is less, to keep the weight on the rooftop low, and therefore the size of plants is limited. The plants are generally set in tubs or other containers, but elaborate roof gardens have been made with small pools and beds. Beds of flowering plants are suitable, among which may be stood tubs of specimen plants to produce a desired effect.

Scented Gardens

Scent is one of the qualities that many people appreciate highly in gardens. Scented gardens, in which scent from leaves or flowers is the main criterion for inclusion of a plant, have been established, especially for the benefit of blind people. Some plants release a strong scent in full sunlight, and many must be bruised or rubbed to yield their fragrance. These are usually grown in raised beds within easy reach of visitors.

Gardening Techniques

Organic Gardening

In plain terms, organic gardening means growing without synthetic fertilizers or pesticides. In larger terms, it is a focus on the larger ecosystem. This type of gardening looks for solutions that improve the health of the soil, the plant, and the animals that surround the garden. Usually this involves a lot of compost and cover crops.

Biodynamic Gardening

This is similar to organic gardening in that it doesn't use any synthetic fertilizers or pesticides, but this is soulful gardening. Beyond a concern for the larger ecosystem, biodynamics look to work in concert with the rhythm of nature both on earth and in the stars. This is a gathering together of many ancient techniques from many cultures. A fundamental concern is the health of the soil using biodynamic composting (often energized, acting like a sort of herbal tea for the garden).

Companion Planting

Companion planting involves the use of plant relationships that encourage prolific growth, and repel or attract insects. In our garden, we plant basil, parsley, and borage among our tomatoes for increased vigor, decreased disease, and more prolific blooming.

Succession Planting

Succession planting involves planting your garden in waves to ensure that there is a crop of a particular vegetable coming on continually through the spring, summer, and fall.

Permaculture

Often done with perennial and native plants, the goal of permaculture is the creation of a self-sustainable system. This type of gardening avoids tilling and synthetic fertilizers and pesticides because the goal is to create a community of plants, soil, people, insects, etc. that work together to keep the garden going without continual disruption.

Hydroponics

Hydroponics is soil-less gardening that involves "rooting" the plants in a continuously circulating liquid fertilizer.

Conventional Gardening

Some gardeners make use of chemical fertilizers, pesticides, and herbicides in varying degrees. The amount just depends on the particular desire of the individual.

Square Foot Gardening

Square foot gardening is small space gardening that takes marks off the garden in square foot increments. This type of gardening attempts to grow plants closer to maximize space and minimize the need for weeding. It also makes use of succession planting.

Mittlieder Method

This is a type of small space (think apartment) gardening that makes use of both soil based and hydroponics techniques. Even more space is saved when this is combined with vertical gardening.

Aquaponics

Aquaponics is gardening in a liquid medium where fish live. This type of gardening makes use of some of the ideas of hydroponics, using living fertilizers that can also be farmed. Very efficient!

Straw Bale

This technique involves gardening in the tops of straw bales instead of tilling the dirt.

Lasagna Gardening

Lasagna gardening involves layering compostable materials, finishing with a layer of dirt on top. Often used for gardening where weeds have gone out of control, the idea is to smother the weeds and create a good, rich soil for the future.

Keyhole Garden

This garden is laid out as a circular raised bed with a path into the circle on one side and a compost pile in the center. The compost pile is usually held in a circle of wire mesh and runs the entire depth of the bed. The compost pile is watered, distributing moisture and nutrients throughout the surrounding bed.

Gardening Tools

Technically to garden all you need is seeds, soils, sun, and water. But a lot of gardening is hard work that it made easier with the right tools. If you're new to gardening and figuring out the basics, there are many gardening tools available that you should consider adding to your collection. I have rounded up some of the most common gardening tools and their uses. What you'll need will be determined by what you grow, where you grow it, and how you grow it, but these tools are great for most gardeners.

Hand Trowel

Whether you're garding in containers, raised beds, or directly in your yard, a hand trowel is a must have tool. Use it to dig, turn up the earth, or pull up stubborn leaves. A hand trowel is actually the first garden tool I bought when we started container gardening on the patio of our apartment, so it is a tool I often recommend for urban gardeners.

Hand trowels are perfect for transferring dirt into pots or planting seedlings and bulbs. Because they're easy to set down and lose track of while you're working in the garden, look for hand tools with bright handles that are easy to spot in the dirt or greenery.

Pruning Shears

This is another tool required no matter how you garden. A lot of cutting and trimming jobs can be handled with a good pair of pruning shears. I find them essential for harvesting herbs, fruits, and vegetables.

They're also great for cutting thick stems and small branches. They're particularly helpful later in summer when vegetable stems and vines are thick. I also use them at the end of the season when I'm cleaning up and putting the garden to bed. They're great for cutting down plants for the compost pile.

Garden Gloves

You may not think of these as a tool, but I find gloves to be an indispensable item in my tool shed. Gloves not only protect your hands from getting dirty but also protect you from injury. If you have to deal with thorny branches or prickly plants, gloves will protect your hands and wrists from scratches, scrapes, and splinters.

If you have sensitive skin like I do, then gardening gloves aren't optional. I have to wear gloves in the garden to avoid rashes and allergic reactions to plants, fertilizers, and other chemicals. Eczema prone gardeners need a nice set of gloves to protect their hands.

They even make touchscreen garden gloves now, which are perfect if you listen to music or podcasts on a smartphone while you garden.

Rake

Rakes are indispensible tools for anyone with a yard. While leaf rakes can be used for a variety of purposes, a bow rake is great to use in the garden. A bow rake can also be used to clear leaves or spread mulch. It's also perfect for leveling soil or breaking up hard garden dirt in the spring.

When we first transitioned from container gardening on a patio to a raised bed community garden, we thought we could just get by with the hand tools we'd used previously. When spring game and it was time to work the dirt and mix in compost, we realized exactly how difficult that was with just hand tools. Another gardener lent us their bow rake to help spread our compost and now we have our own to use in the garden. This is must have for yards, raised beds, or even community garden plots.

Digging Shovel

If you're gardening in your yard or a raised bed, you'll find that a digging shovel is an extremely useful tool. Not only can you use it to dig holes, it's also great for transporting dirt from a wheelbarrow to your garden without having to dump the whole load.

Shovels are also great for stirring compost piles or mixing potting soil before you add it to your containers. If you need to create a garden or level ground, a sturdy shovel is perfect for turning dirt or removing it. Look for pointed shovels, like the one pictured, for digging. If you find regular shovels are too heavy, some designs are made of lightweight materials but are still perfect for digging in gardens.

Garden Spade

While you may have all of your digging needs taken care of by a hand trowel and a digging shovel, you may find a garden spade to be extremely helpful in your garden bed.

Designed to use in tight spaces, the square-shaped blade is perfect for digging holes for plants and bushes, especially in established gardens where you don't want to disturb existing plants. I also love them for removing weeds that have deep root systems I can't pull out by hand. If you have a perennial you need to transplant, a spade is perfect to "cut out" the plant from the dirt and then dig a new hole for it.

Since it's essentially like a shovel, you can also use it for transporting dirt and general digging in your yard or garden bed.

Garden Hoe

We always get a lot of use out of our hoe in the spring when we're preparing the garden for planting. The blade is perfect for weeding, easily chopping through unwanted growth and and clearing it out of your garden beds. You can also use it to spread compost in tight spaces.

The type of hoe and the size and shape of the blade will be determined by the type of gardening you do. If you're dealing with large areas of dirt or vegetable gardens, you may need a wider hoe. For flower gardens, a delicate blade may work better.

Choose a blade width based on your needs, you may even want to buy multiple hoes of different sizes to handle a bigger variety of projects.

Hose + Spray Nozzles

Unless all of your plants are in self-watering containers, you're going to need to water your garden. While some urban gardeners can get away with just a watering can, if you have a yard then a garden hose will be the best way to water your plants. While traditional hoses are still very common, we recommend a light-weight expandable hose that is easier to maneuver.

In addition to a hose, make sure you get an adjustable spray nozzle. These not only help you control the water so you aren't wasting any water between your garden beds, but they also help you control the way the water is delivered. Many spray nozzles have adjustable spray patterns, allowing you to mist newly planted seeds and seedlings while soaking established plants like tomatoes or flower bushes that need lots of water in the heat of summer.

Wheelbarrow

If you're lucky enough to have a nice big yard to garden in, you'll find that a wheelbarrow or a garden cart will make a lot of jobs so much easier. Move dirt, compost, even piles of leaves effortlessly across your property. They're also great for transporting new seedlings to your garden bed.

A traditional wheelbarrow design will be best if you're often moving soil or compost as it's easy to dump your load once you read your destination. If you mostly need to move tools or plants then a cart design might work better for you.

Loppers

If you have trees or shrubs that ever need pruning, a simple pair of pruning shears won't cut it (hah!). Loppers are perfect for keeping your hedges under control or removing diseased branches.

A nice pair of loppers (like the one pictured) will allow you to cut branches up to 1-2″ in diameter. When you're shopping, make sure to pay attention to the max thickness the loppers will cut. Usually, longer loppers can cut thicker branches. If can afford the extra cost, buy one that can handle 2″ branches.

Weeder

Weeds are the bane of an gardener's existence and can be a major pain to remove. Luckily there are a few handy tools to use to battle weeds in your garden. The first is a hand weeder (pictured), which some call a dandelion digger. It's designed to help remove weeds with a tap root, with the tines penetrating the soil to easily pull the weed out.

Hori Hori Garden Knife

Sometimes referred to as a garden knife, the hori hori originated in Japan, but has become popular with gardeners across the world. It's a stainless steel blade that is slightly curved with a sharp edge and a serrated edge. That makes it perfect for cutting through soil or roots. Some people even use it as a weeder.

Some people use a hori hori instead of a hand trowel, as you can easily use it to transplant seedlings and dig holes for planting. Many models also have measurements engraved in the blade, making it easy to measure depth when planting seeds. Campers also find a hori hori useful for digging into hard packed dirt or prying up rocks under your tent.

Spading Fork

You may recognize a spading fork as a digging fork, garden fork, or a graip. Similar in appearance to a pitchfork, a spading fork is meant for turning dirt and soil. Usually it has four sturdy tines perfect for loosening hard dirt and lifting soil. It's also nice to mix fresh compost into established beds.

It's called a spading fork because there are some scenarios where it works better than a traditional spade since it's perfect for raking out weeds or breaking up clumps of dirt in tight spaces in already established gardens.

Available in full size or handheld models, pick one that works best for the size of your garden. Container gardeners will do just fine with a handheld spading fork, but those with raised beds or traditional garden beds may find a full-size tool will work best.

Pruning Saw

If you have branches too thick for your lopper to cut, then a pruning saw is the tool you need. These tools are the middle ground between a lopper and a handsaw or chain saw. The one pruning saw pictures can cut through branches of to 8 inches thick, perfect for pruning trees in your yard. You can also use it for shrubs and plants.

If you're trying to minimize the number of garden tools you own, I'd recommend getting a good pair of pruning shears and a pruning saw and just skip the loppers. While you may need to take care of most of your branch cutting needs with your handsaw, the design of pruning saws is perfect for slicing off branches in tight spaces, especially when dealing with small trees and shrubs.

Edger

As you might guess from the name, an edger is meant to create edges in your garden. An edger is used to cut a clean line in the soil between grass and a sidewalk, driveway, or a garden bed. They're generally designed in a half circle shape with a lip on the top where you can press the tool down with your foot. To use the tool, you place the blade where you want to create the edge and then step down to cut into the soil and rock the edger side to side before moving down to repeat the steps.

An edger is a specialized tool that doesn't have a lot of uses, but if you want to create clearly defined lines in your yard, it's the perfect way to separate the grass from your garden. The created lines will make your yard and pathways look tidy and well planned.

How To Choose Your Modern Garden

How to choose a garden overwhelming because of not being sure on how to tell which type of garden layout is the best kind for you?

Don't get stressed out over it. Sit down with a notebook and a pen and think about some of these factors that will help you determine what type of garden is the best fit for you.

How much land do you have to devote to a garden?

Will your garden cover your entire back yard or front yard, or just a portion of your yard? Do you want a small, tidy garden or a large sprawling garden? Many people think they want a huge garden until they realize how much work goes into making a big garden beautiful. If you are just a beginning gardener you may want to start small and not invest a lot of time or money into your garden until you're sure it's something you want to stick with.

How much gardening experience do you have?

If you are not an experienced gardener you will have a lot to learn. On how to choose a garden it may be best to start with a smaller garden that will allow you to start over if you make mistakes. A smaller garden will also make it easier for you to practice getting soil PH levels correct to grow plants and to experiment with different fertilizers, composting, and mulches to see what works the best in your particular type of soil.

How much time can you realistically spend caring for your garden?

There's nothing worse than having an untended garden. If you don't have enough time to properly care for and nurture a huge garden then maybe you should plant a small garden unless you can afford to hire someone to care for the garden when you can't. You could also lose a lot of money if your plants die from neglect. If you are an experienced gardener who has lots of time to devote to a garden then you can probably handle having a very large garden where someone who is new to gardening or has health issues or time issues may not be able to.

Are you physically able to garden?

Gardening might not seem like it would be very physically difficult but it can be tough to spend a lot of time doing repetitive tasks like planting, weeding, watering, and other garden chores. Even though gardening is gentle physical activity, it is still physical activity and it might be tough for some people who have joint problems, arthritis, or other degenerative conditions to garden on a regular basis. You don't have to be super fit to garden, but you do need to be able to perform the basic physical tasks associated with gardening.

If you do have trouble moving around or being in the same position for a long time then you might want to know how to choose a garden that doesn't require a lot of upkeep, like a Wildflower garden, so that you can still have a beautiful garden but physically taking care of the garden won't be so hard for you to do.

Simple Gardening Tips for Beginners

Not everyone has a green thumb, but that shouldn't stop you from pursuing gardening. Fresh fruits, vegetables, herbs and flowers make a yard brighter and can help you to eat healthy on a budget. But if you're a first-time gardener, there are a lot of things you need to know before you grow.

Know what to Grow

Successful gardening starts with knowing which crops are viable where you live. The USDA's plant hardiness zone map indicates the 11 different climate zones in America measured by the average annual extreme minimum temperature. Seed packaging and plant labels will tell you what grows best in your area.

Know where to Grow

Knowing what you want to grow will help you decide where in your yard is the best place for a garden. Some plants like direct sunlight, while others prefer shade. Check your plant package for this information.

Test your Soil

To make sure your soil is healthy enough to foster plants, send a sample to the lab or use an at-home kit to measure the pH level of your land. Different fruits and vegetables can tolerate varying pH levels, but generally speaking anywhere from 6.5 to 7 will do (except for eggplant, melons and potatoes). It's also important to test for these three nutrients: nitrogen, potassium and phosphorus. If your test yields bad results, you'll have to take some time to correct the deficiencies.

Consider Raised Beds

Being new to gardening, you want to set yourself up for success and a raised garden bed may be the best way to do that, even though it might take more investment up front. You will have more control over soil in a raised garden bed as well as simpler weed and pest control. I always advise beginner gardeners to build raised beds; they are really helpful when it comes to separating plants according to their needs. In raised beds, you can grow different sets of plants, all grouped in separate patches.

Map it Out

Now that you know what your soil is like, what kind of plants you should grow and where you are going to put your new garden, spend some time mapping it out before you break ground. This will help you double-check that you are optimizing your space properly.

Get Some Gear

Without the right tools, or any tools at all, you can run into a serious mess quickly. Some essentials include breathable water-resistant gloves, pruners, loppers, a garden fork, a hand trowel, a spade, a rake, a hoe, a hose with an adjustable nozzle, a watering wand or watering can and a wheelbarrow.

Use Seed Starter Kits

An easy, almost guaranteed way of getting your plant to sprout is by using a seed starter kit. These single or multiple use trays provide perfect conditions for your crop to germinate. This allows you to begin the growing process inside when it's too early to plant outside, and then put it in the ground later when it's nice enough.

Start Small

Taking care of your plants requires time and dedication. It's easy to get carried away with the excitement of growing everything under the sun, but it's best to start small so you can care for each individual plant as best you can.

Label Everything in Your Garden

Even if you've only planted three different types of seeds, it's a good idea to label what it is and where you planted it, because it's easy to forget.

Utilize Companion Planting

Companion planting is growing different crops in the same vicinity for a variety of reasons including maximizing use of space, providing nutrients and warding off pests. Some species thrive when they are planted close together, while others can actually stunt each other's growth. For example, tomatoes produce greater yields (and keep away mosquitos and flies) when they coexist with basil. Other tomato allies include asparagus, carrots, celery, onions, lettuce, marigold, parsley and spinach. As far as enemies go, keep tomatoes away from cabbage, beets, corn, fennel, dill, potatoes and rosemary.

Don't Plant Things Too Close Together

Like people, plants have personal space bubbles. They need enough room to grow properly, and if other crops are too close they can stunt growth and spread disease unless they're companion plants.

Mix it up

You don't have to restrict yourself to just growing vegetables or just growing herbs. Feel free to mix it up when it comes to your plants. Go ahead and plant those herbs in your veggie garden. There are some plants that are natural companions and do not necessarily yield the same crop.

Use Compost

Compost is organic material that can be added to your garden to help your plants grow. This can be anything from eggshells, tea bags and coffee grounds to ashes, lawn trimmings and fur. Adding these things to your soil helps it to retain moisture, fight pests and disease, and stimulate good bacterial growth. Also, finding ways to reuse your waste lowers your carbon footprint.

Use Fertilizer

Even if you decide composting isn't your thing, you still shouldn't skip enhancing the soil. Fertilizing the ground is an important step to add nutrients and minerals.

Keep Watering Needs in Mind

When you are plotting out your garden, also keep in mind how much each of the plants needs in terms of amount of water and frequency of watering, then make sure to match like to like.

Get Rid of Weeds

Planting is only the beginning of the work on your new garden. You need to keep weeds out. Weeds are bad for your garden because they compete with the plants you are trying to grow for the nutrients in the soil as well as valuable garden space.

Mulch may be your Best Friend

Depending on what you are growing, you may want to consider mulch. Mulch helps to feed the soil with nutrients and protects against erosion. Mulch will also help your new garden fend off weeds.

Be Patient

Growing plants takes time, so remain calm and be patient while you get your garden up and going.

Organize Your Seeds

To make sure seeds stay neat and don't get lost or thrown away, find a way to properly store the packets. One creative option is to drop them in the sleeves of a small photo album. This way, you can turn the pages and see exactly what you've got and they're protected.

Store Your Seeds Correctly

Keeping your seeds viable means storing them correctly. Keep seeds at a constant temperature as well as a constant humidity. Ideally a seed should be stored at a temperature below 50 degrees Fahrenheit and at less than 50 percent humidity.

Practice Crop Rotation

What you grow has a direct effect on the soil surrounding it. Growing the same plant in the same spot every year will mean you are depleting the same nutrients every year. Crop rotation can help you replenish nutrients in the soil throughout your garden. Crop rotation will also keep common pests on their toes because their food source will change location year after year. Instead of doing a basil plant year after year, consider planting some plants and flowers you didn't know were edible.

PATIO GARDENING

What is a Patio Gardening

Patio Gardening is quite literally gardening in the premise of one's patios. Containers are often the most neat and efficient way. But if there is soil under your patio there are some creative ways to still garden straight in-geound.

To reiterate, while containers are often the most practical choice for patio gardens they are not the definition nor are they the rule. Patio gardening is one of the healthiest hobbies you can have.

How to Make a Patio Garden Plan

If you want to add some color, amazing fragrance, and beauty to your patio, why not create a patio garden?

This is really quite simple to do once you have a patio garden plan in place. Start off by deciding what you intend to use your patio garden for, how you will plant the area, what practical components you need to consider, and what plants, furniture, and pavers you will select. Of course, you'll also need to think about a theme or design for your garden.

The three most important considerations that any patio garden plan should begin with includes:

- Ambience that you want to create
- Garden's purpose or function
- How to maximize small spaces

Once you have all of that determined, you can move on to the actual purchasing of items and physical labor to put it all together.

Ambience of a Patio Garden

Most home gardeners design a patio garden that features a quiet place to get away and relax. What this aspect involves depends on what you have to start with. Eyesores can be hidden behind plants, trellises, and hanging baskets. Patio furniture can be added for a quiet place to sit and relax. Pavers can be used to create a theme, design, or borders for your garden. The plants, containers, furniture, and pavers are typically selected to match your chosen function of the garden.

Function or Purpose of Your Patio Garden

If you have lots of sun and a container, then you'll do great growing rosemary.

The basic premise of a patio garden is that you are going to use it to grow herbs, vegetables, fruits, flowers, or some combination of these. In addition to this, you need to decide whether you are going to create a garden solely to sustain your kitchen by growing vegetables, growing a combination of vegetables and herbs, or growing a simple herb garden.

You might decide to use it for some other purpose including an outdoor eating area, an entertaining spot for dinner parties, a place to relax with friends socially, or a family area for relaxing and bonding together. No matter which garden design you intend to make use of, you are probably going to want to include some type of gardening strategy aimed at offering itself as a form of insect repellent in order to keep pests away.

The size of your patio is going to limit exactly what you can do with it to some extent. However, with some careful planning and strategizing, you can create a patio that meets as many of your intentions as you like. You can incorporate more than one purpose simply by dividing your patio garden into more than one open area and using a variety of space-saving gardening strategies.

How to Maximize Small Spaces in a Patio Garden Plan

You can maximize small spaces by planting smaller varieties, limiting the number of varieties that you grow, utilizing companion planting, limiting the number of plants for each variety, using container gardening, practicing vertical gardening, and raised bed planting. One of the benefits of each of these types of gardening is that it makes good use of small spaces efficiently and easily.

Planting smaller varieties can save space since you can use smaller containers or take up less ground. If you limit the number of varieties that you grow, you can reduce how much space you need to plant your veggies and herbs. If you utilize companion planting, you can combine more than one variety of vegetable or herb in a single container or plot of ground saving space. Following that train of thought, if you limit the number of plants for each variety of plant, you can save on the space needed for planting.

Using container gardening strategies allows you to use every nook and cranny of the garden since you can find planters, baskets, and boxes in so many different sizes from large to tiny. Today's technology has even made it possible to plant in those hard-to-get-to spots by giving us self-watering planters and containers. If you practice vertical gardening, you can grow vining plants such as cucumbers and beans upward rather than along the ground.

Raised bed planting involves a bit of work since you need to construct a box for planting and growing. However, this practice makes it possible to grow vegetables, herbs, and flowers in locations that were once unusable for gardeners. A variation of the traditional raised bed design is the elevated patio garden design. This strategy offers a unique method of gardening that does not involve tearing up the ground, but rather incorporates the use of a garden bench, table, or elevated planter for gardening purposes. It is perfect for individuals who have difficulty bending or kneeling down on the ground, including those who are handicapped.

Patio Design with Pavers and Furniture

Depending on your existing patio and its condition, you might need or want to incorporate patio pavers to define certain areas or create pathways throughout the garden. Patio pavers are durable and easy to repair should they get damaged. While brick pavers have been the most popular style, several others are available allowing you to create your own sense of style in your patio garden. Of course, if you don't have a patio yet, you can use pavers to create a durable floor for it.

Once you decide the primary use of your patio, you can set about staging it with furniture. If you are using your patio garden primarily for dining purposes, you should look for a set of patio chairs and table. Pick a size that is going to be large enough for your typical gathering event.

If your patio garden is designed primarily for relaxation, then you can eliminate the table and select a variety of patio chairs. If you prefer, you can include a patio glider or sofa that will accommodate more than one individual at a time. If small children are going to frequent the patio garden, consider purchasing furniture intentionally designed for small children.

If you have a pre-determined wall or corner area, you can incorporate built-in seating in that area. This allows you to keep the remaining portion of your patio open for other uses. Consider incorporating container gardening along the remaining perimeter of your patio as well as at the ends of each seating arrangement.

You can create dramatic and elegant focal points using fountains, garden urns, spiral herb gardens, or fancy companion gardening containers. One of the benefits of this type of garden is that it only takes a few minutes to change the entire look of your patio garden by moving your furniture and planters around.

Selecting Patio Garden Plants

When you are still in the planning stages, you should carefully consider how much of the patio receives full sun, partial sun, and no sun. If you want to have a successful crop, then you need to select plants that can do well given the conditions that you have.

It is important to take note of where the sun shines when gardening on a patio. Certain plants require full sun for 6 to 8 hours a day so it is important to ensure that they obtain this amount for a healthy growing season. One of the benefits to container gardening is your ability to move plants around from place to place to give them a chance at a bit more sunshine. If this is not an optimal strategy for you, it is best to choose plants that can do well given the conditions that you have. If you do intend to move your containers to catch as much sun as possible, make sure that you purchase ones that are lightweight and easy to move.

If the existing soil near your patio is unsuitable for growing, you can create your own mix using soil, compost, and fertilizer purchased from the store. Raised beds, elevated beds, and container gardening can all be used to make up for poor soil conditions.

You can either water your patio garden on a regular basis, use self-watering planters, or use a combination of both methods to provide your plants with the moisture they need.

Design your garden so that you have low-maintenance plants around the borders. Mulching provides protection from too much or too little heat while also retaining moisture. Consider using a weed-resistant cloth beneath the mulch to reduce the need to weed. Perennials are perfect choices when selecting low-maintenance plants for your garden.

You can create a border for your patio using a cluster of containers in different shapes and sizes. Use a variety of plants for a nice visual effect. Alternatively, you can use a row of identical containers. Just remember to plant a variety of vegetables and herbs or you will be eating the same type of produce each night.

Use tall plants to hide less-attractive areas of the yard or views. If you are close to a noisy highway, the thicker your growth, the better it will block out the noise.

Design your garden so that you have low-maintenance plants around the borders. Mulching provides protection from too much or too little heat while also retaining moisture. Consider using a weed-resistant cloth beneath the mulch to reduce the need to weed. Perennials are perfect choices when selecting low-maintenance plants for your garden.

You can create a border for your patio using a cluster of containers in different shapes and sizes. Use a variety of plants for a nice visual effect. Alternatively, you can use a row of identical containers. Just remember to plant a variety of vegetables and herbs or you will be eating the same type of produce each night.

Use tall plants to hide less-attractive areas of the yard or views. If you are close to a noisy highway, the thicker your growth, the better it will block out the noise.

Select fragrant colorful varieties that your guests will find enjoyable to look at as well as smell. Scented plants such as lavender attract beneficial insects. Herbs are terrific for repelling unwanted insects from the area.

If you plan to host dinner parties, plant a wide variety of produce either in containers or a raised bed that you can cook with or make a salad from. Add is some herbs for an added taste of flavor.

Designing Patio Gardens with Dining Patios

If one of the primary purposes of your outdoor garden/patio area is to enjoy dining among the beauty of your plants, then you need to take a look at how much room you are going to have left once you place your table and chairs. In order not to have to sacrifice room that could be used for growing, consider purchasing a table with storage areas built into it.

This provides a handy set up for storing essential garden tools without sacrificing room that is better suited for growing. Since you limit your space, also consider relying on vertical and container gardening. You can purchase seating that includes hidden storage compartments. These storage areas can be used to store cushions or garden tools.

Soften the edges of your patio area, especially near your entertaining or dining area by planting a variety of herbs and/or flowers. What you select primarily depends on whether you want herbs to sprinkle on your food or flowers to brighten up your gathering.

Designing a Family Patio Garden

If your patio garden is going to be used by all members of the family, you need to design it in a way that it is functional for everyone. Plant some taller plants or use vertical gardening to provide shade for the very young as well as for anyone who prefers to get in out of the sunshine. Plant a variety of herbs to repel insects so that you can have a relaxing environment for family gatherings.

Set a small portion of the patio apart for a children's garden and plant hardy plants such as tomatoes so that your children can enjoy gardening with a high likelihood of having something to show for it. Include an area for adults and older children to garden planting vegetables if you want fresh produce and flowers if you want color and fragrance.

Social or Entertaining Patio Garden Designs

If your patio is utilized mainly for entertaining and socializing, you can design it for privacy as well as for beauty. In order to create natural privacy, you can plant a small grouping of trees provided you have the soil to do so. If you are confined to concrete or macadam, a user-friendly alternative is to take advantage of vertical gardening so that your plants grow up toward the sky rather than along the ground. Not only will this type of gardening provide you with some privacy, but you'll be able to enjoy fresh fruits and vegetables throughout the growing season.

Design lounging areas so that they enjoy partial shade at least part of the day. This will avoid the need to relocate your furniture. If you already have or intend to get a hot tub, an herb garden offers an excellent way to repel unwanted insects without resorting to harsh chemicals. Trellis panels can provide the same semblance of privacy as a patio wall. Plus, they offer a finished look to the area. The trellis should have a finish that blends well with your patio garden whether you are using container, vertical, or raised bed gardening.

Designing L-shaped Patio Gardens

Many urban patios are L-shaped, limiting what you can do with them. With the clever use of your space, you can create a peaceful resting spot as well as a dining area. You can have a wall put in along the border to provide some privacy as well as definition to the patio area. Make sure that the wall is painted white to provide an added touch of brightness. You can plant along the side of the wall using raised beds, an elevated garden design, or containers.

For an outdoor patio garden, planting several vegetables using the vertical method of gardening along the walls can save space while providing you with fresh cucumbers, string beans, peas, and cherry tomatoes. Use the narrowest end of the patio for benches, a glider, or several chairs for relaxation. The wider end of the patio can be used for outdoor dining.

Patio Gardening in Containers

If you find yourself wanting to experience the joys of gardening but think that you don't have enough room because you don't have a real yard, you should consider container patio gardening. It allows you to make use of the space that you do have to create a small mini-garden full of nutritious herbs, vegetables, and fruit along with a bevy of colorful flowers.

Choosing Patio Garden Containers

One of the most important considerations during your planning stages is determining the type of containers that you are going to use for your container patio garden. Since you can select almost any size container in almost any shape and made out of almost any material for your patio garden, you have lots of options. It is important to consider a few points regarding how much time you want to spend in the garden, whether you want to create a theme for your garden, and how large of a container patio garden you want to create.

Choosing Container Sizes

The size of the container that you select is going to depend on two main facets — what type of plant are you growing in the container and the location where the container is going to be placed. You need to select a container that is going to be large enough to hold a growing plant while being the proper size to fit in the spot that you need to place it.

Containers with a five-gallon capacity are going to be the most useful for your gardening needs as far as most vegetables are concerned. Smaller containers in the one to two gallon range are best used for herbs, leaf lettuce, and radishes.

You want to select a container that is going to be roomy enough to allow your plants to grow properly without being so large that they appear out of place. For roomy areas of your patio garden, you can select wooden half barrels, plastic tubs, bushel baskets, large drums, planter boxes, and ceramic pots.

Some of your vegetables need deep containers to grow properly while other varieties can make do with a shallow container. For example, radishes and green onions can grow nicely in a shallow container whereas carrots and potatoes do best when growing in containers that are deep.

Choosing Porous versus Nonporous Containers

Another consideration that you must think about is whether or not you want to use porous or nonporous containers. Nonporous containers are going to retain moisture better than porous ones. If your patio takes in a lot of sun, this is an important consideration for you. Either way, you need to provide adequate drainage for your containers. If they do not have drainage holes set into them, you need to make them. For the best results, place a few drainage holes about ¼ to ½ inch above the container's bottom on the sides of the container so that it can drain freely when necessary. Adding a proper lining of gravel or coarse pebbles in the bottom of the container is also beneficial to the plants.

Types of Patio Garden Containers

Wood planters are sold in cedar, teak, and redwood. Each of these woods is durable, rot-resistant, and long-lasting. Offering a natural color, wooden planters blend well in most gardens. Wooden trellises can easily be combined with wooden planters to create a space for vertical planting. The use of plastic liners and drainage holes will extend the life of your wooden planters. You can treat your planters with a waterproofing agent, paint, or a non-toxic stain to extend their life.

Terracotta pots are sold in true terracotta as well as faux terracotta. Terracotta planters are porous so they dry out faster increasing the need to water your plants more frequently. Try to purchase terracotta pots that are thicker to minimize chipping and cracking. Since terracotta planters are among the heavier ones, they withstand windy conditions quite well. Their warm, earthy tones blend well in most gardens.

Ceramic planters include a wide variety of earthenware, stoneware, and glazed planters.

Since ceramic planters are nonporous, they tend to retain moisture longer minimizing your watering needs. If your patio containers are going to be exposed to low temperatures, you should look for ceramic planters that have been labeled as frost or freezing resistant. Since ceramic planters are sold in an attractive assortment of colors, using them for your plants is a great way to add extra color or blend a theme in your garden.

Concrete planters are more traditional in style. They are also heavier and more difficult to move around, so you might want to consider your purchase carefully. However, this makes them a great choice for patio gardens that are exposed to windy conditions.

If you decide to use concrete planters, you need to seal them to minimize damage due to weather and soil. Of course, you can always purchase faux concrete planters and avoid the need to use any treatments to protect the planters. Fiberglass, fiberstone, and resin planters are easy-to-care-for making them an easy choice for the patio gardener with limited time.

Stone planters offer the same traditional look as concrete planters, and are just as heavy if they are made from natural stone. Faux stone and fiberstone styles are not as heavy as true stone or concrete and so they make more sense for patios that are suspended into the air such as those found attached to apartments and condos. If your patio garden is located in an area where heavy winds are going to occur, choose heavier planters that can handle the wind.

Although wall planters are attractive and can be used to save valuable ground-level space, your use of them is going to be limited to whatever walls are present in the patio area. Since these walls typically include windows and a door, you need to make your selection carefully with size and style in mind so that your wall planter looks good wherever you position it without looking out of place. Wall planters are sold in an assortment of styles and materials including cast iron, wrought iron, wood, and terracotta.

Metal planters are attractive, shiny, and stylish. This type of planter is perfect for lounging patios or those on which you intend to do quite a bit of entertaining. Metal planters are sold in copper, wrought iron, zinc, and stainless steel. They hold up well to the elements of weather and require little care. They can also be used as "cache" pots, which means that they hold a smaller planter that is often less attractive. This avoids the need to fill the metal planter with soil.

Self-watering planters are perfect for the gardener who has limited time to spend tending to his garden. Even though you must supply the water occasionally, you need to do so far less frequently than you would when watering plants. Self-watering planters are perfect for those hard-to-reach areas of a container patio garden. This style of container is a bit more expensive, but the convenience you get is well worth the price. You can find an attractive assortment of styles including hanging baskets and terrazzo models.

Window boxes can be used to add a touch of color to your apartment or house walls while also giving you added space for gardening. Window boxes are sold in different sizes, styles, and materials. Wrought iron, fiberglass, hayrack, and wrought iron are among the most popular materials used to craft window boxes.

Garden urns are sold in a wide variety of materials including stone, concrete, resin, and terracotta. They offer a decorative way to showcase your favorite plants, placing them well above the ground.

A growing market of unique planters features some clever designs. If you are planning your container patio garden with a contemporary look, you might want to include uniquely designed planters that portray modern themes, shapes such as mailboxes, and split pots.

Growing Vegetables in Containers on the Patio Garden

Although just about any vegetable that you can grow in a traditional garden can be grown in a container patio garden within reason, it is important to consider just how much space you have when you select your plants so that you can choose wisely.

You should stay away from vining plants unless you intend to use vertical gardening strategies. A trellis, fence, or vegetable cage can be used to support your vining plants so they grow above the container rather than trailing over it. Vining vegetables that you might want to consider since they typically produce bountiful crops include: cucumbers and pole beans. You'll want to plant such varieties near any fences or walls in order to keep your garden looking neat and attractive.

Vegetables that are well-suited for container gardening include: tomatoes, peppers, leaf lettuce, squash, beans, green onions, mini-carrots, and radishes. It is important to consider the type of vegetable that you are planting when you select your containers. The following chart provides a handy guide with suggested container size for various vegetables.

Vegetable	# of Plants	Container Size	Suggested Varieties
Broccoli	1 plant	2 gallons	Bonanza, Packman, any
Carrot	2-3 plants	1 gallon	Baby Spike, Little Finger, Scarlet Nantes
Cucumber	1 plant	1 gallon	Burpless, Crispy, Early Pick, Liberty, Salty
Beans	2-3 plants	2 gallons	Blue Lake, Contender, Kentucky Wonder
Onions	3-5	1 gallon	Evergreen

			Bunching, Beltsville Bunching
Leaf Lettuce	2 plants	1 gallon	Buttercrunch, Romaine, Bibb, Ruby
Pepper	1-2 plants	5 gallons	Jalapeno, Keystone Resistant
Radish	3-5 plants	1 gallon	Scarlet Globe
Tomato	1 plant	5 gallons	Patio, Toy Boy, Saladette

Growing Herbs in Containers on the Patio Garden

Selecting the herbs that you are going to plant depends on how you intend to use them. If you intend to use herbs to sustain your kitchen's cooking needs, then you should plant them where they are readily accessible such as closest to the door. The easier it is to harvest your herbs, the more likely it is that you will use them regularly.

Most herbs require a minimum of 4 to 6 hours of sunlight each day. Container-grown herbs accommodate any size patio. Edible herb container gardens are those that include a variety of herbs for use in salads, cooking, and teas. It is one of the most popular garden designs. Planting an herb garden according to a theme is popular. The idea is to plant herbs that accommodate your style of cooking.

One example is to grow an Italian herb garden that includes oregano, basil, rosemary, and parsley. An Asian herb garden includes lemon grass and cilantro. A French herb garden includes thyme, tarragon, marjoram, chervil, and fennel. A Mexican herb garden consists of lemon verbena, spearmint, sweet basil, and bay.

Growing Flowers in Containers on the Patio Garden

Flowers are the perfect addition to any container patio garden. Not only do they add a nice touch of color, but they also provide sweet fragrances. Just imagine a bevy of lush foliage and bright blossoms cascading over your patio containers

One of your most important considerations is to select the proper container for the type of flowers that you plant. For example, trailing flowers should be planted in hanging baskets. Next, you need to follow proper planting instructions as provided with the specific plants that you select. This includes selecting the proper size container, soil, and fertilizer.

If you live in an all-season area, then annuals or plants that survive through one growing season only are going to be your best choice. One of the benefits of using annuals is that you can choose new flowers each year, changing the appearance of your garden almost effortlessly. Annuals that are well-suited for container growing include begonias, marigolds, salvias, petunias, and caladiums.

You can use flowers in a vegetables and herb container garden to attract beneficial insects including pollinators to your garden in order to create an optimal growing environment. Simply incorporate them into your patio using separate containers. In the case of marigolds, you can even include them in containers with certain vegetables through companion planting.

Companion Planting within Containers

Companion planting combines two or more varieties of plants together that grow well together. Typically, the combination reduces pest infestation and treatment. This occurs because some plants attract beneficial insects while others repel harmful ones.

The pairing of plants is critical to the success of companion planting. It is important to combine sun-loving plants with tall growth with shade-loving plants with a shorter height. In this way, they each get what they need without infringing on the other.

If several varieties of plants are going to share one container, then the container needs to be sufficiently large to accommodate all of them. Choose your container wisely, making sure that it provides sufficient growth for each variety of plant that you include.

Vegetable	Gets Along Well With	Does Not Get Along Well With
Beans	Carrots, cabbage, cucumbers, marigolds	Chives, garlic, leeks
Beets	Lettuce, onions, sage	Pole beans
Broccoli	Celery, dill, rosemary	Strawberries, oregano
Cabbage	Oregano, sage, potato	Strawberries, tomatoes
Carrots	Beans, lettuce, peas, onions, radishes	Radishes, chives, parsnips, dill
Cauliflower	Celery, beans, oregano	Peas, potato, strawberries
Cucumber	Beans, peas, lettuce, celery, radishes	Potatoes, cauliflower, basil
Lettuce	Carrots, strawberries, celery	Beans, parsley

Onions	Broccoli, cabbage, strawberries, tomatoes, lettuce	Peas, beans
Peas	Beans, carrots, cucumbers, radishes	Onions
Potatoes	Beans, cabbage, peas	Cucumbers, squash
Tomato	Carrots, celery, parsley, marigolds	Potatoes, fennel

Raised Beds on the Patio Garden

Why use Raised Beds?

Creating raised beds around an outdoor patio garden may seem like more trouble than it's worth. After all, you can use small containers, trellises and so many other forms of gardening on a patio. But raised beds can reward your time and effort with better drainage, easier growing, better harvesting and most of all convenience for many gardeners.

Raised beds are especially popular with gardeners who have knee or back problems, or who are elderly or disabled. They make a good companion to existing container gardens on a patio, as they have similar watering and fertilizing needs.

Since you'll have complete control over the soil that goes into the beds, you also can be sure it is free of rocks, well-mixed, and rich with organic matter. Raised beds provide a structural limitation to weeds and pests, and allow plants to root deeply for better growth and health. They are ideal for patio gardeners, as they create a little garden directly on the patio where you can grow just about anything you want.

Types of Raised Beds

Raised beds can be placed in a number of locations, whether it is in a rooftop patio garden, just off your ground-level patio, or even on top of rock or concrete. Consider what type of raised bed will work best for your patio garden before beginning.

Here are some raised bed ideas:

If you are simply planting a variety of herbs for a little kitchen garden on your patio, choose half-barrel planters used in landscaping to give the herbs vertical drainage yet limited surface area, as several herbs can be invasive and should be given limited space. Walled raised beds will be the most common for patio gardeners, as they are quite versatile and can be built out of a variety of materials to match your patio or home.

Building a Raised Bed Garden

Make sure when planning your raised beds that they will be made of a non-toxic material that won't leach chemicals into your plants' roots. Stone, cinder blocks or bricks are common raised bed materials, and untreated lumber is another choice for those who are handy with carpentry. All of these should be available at garden or home improvement stores, and the stone and brick options come in a variety of shapes and colors for gardeners who want to have their beds match their patio or outdoor furniture.

Be sure if you are using lumber that you secure the corners of the boards well with braces, screws or reinforced blocks. There also are raised bed kits or snap-together frames available, which sometimes have the benefit of being easily taken apart for movement or storage. A popular material for raised beds in backyard gardens is old railroad ties, but these may be too large for use on a patio. However, most lumber and home improvement stores sell cut lumber in nice four-foot and smaller lengths, making it easy to replicate this look on your patio.

Designing a Raised Bed Garden on the Patio

Most raised beds should be between one and two feet high, but make them a height that you will find easy to work with, so that you don't have to bend or kneel as much. As for width, if the bed is accessible from both sides, you can make them as wide as four feet, assuming you can reach two feet in from each side. If they are only reachable on one side, don't make them much wider than two feet, as it will become difficult to reach in and tend the farthest plants. Rectangular shapes are the easiest to build, but you may choose other shapes based on your patio design and DIY capabilities

Note that the location should be well leveled first so that the bed isn't deeper on one side than the other. Check it with a level first to be sure all the water won't drain to one side. Many gardeners also prefer to line the bottom of raised beds with black plastic or landscaping cloth to keep weeds from growing up through the bottom of the bed. If your bed is taller than about two feet, you will want to provide more support for the walls.

When using wood, you can drill holes vertically down through the wall, and insert stakes, rebar or other sturdy supports to keep the walls standing straight and even over time. When using brick or stone, be sure to mortar uneven stones and set uniform blocks offset from one row to the next, for better stability.

Placement of Your Raised Bed Patio Garden

Of course, you'll want to place your raised beds in an attractive location around your patio, not just haphazardly. But while you're considering placement, also choose a sunny location. Most plants will benefit from full sun, and will need it to produce their full potential at harvesting time. For maximum landscaping effect, try creating different heights, sizes and shapes of beds. You could, for instance, create a low, border-style bed to the outside of your taller main bed. Or, plan on growing your flowers in one raised bed as a focal point to draw the eye, and allowing smaller surrounding beds to grow vegetables and herbs.

Try to place plants you know will grow taller to the middle of the bed, and low, ground-level plants on the outsides, for ease of watering and tending throughout the season. One no-no for raised beds on your patio, however, is to build them right up against the house or shed. This will attract moisture– and eventually rot –to the side of the building, and shade the bed more than is healthy for most plants.

Soil and Water for Raised Bed Patio Gardens

In raised beds, you need a lighter soil than in the garden, similar to container gardening. If you already have a soil mix that you use for other containers on your patio, the same mix is good to use in raised beds as well. If not, choose a soil mix that is loose, rich in organic matter, and lightened with mulch, vermiculite or peat moss. It should be well-mixed, not layered.

Throughout the season, pay attention to the soil moisture. Raised beds on patios will dry out more quickly than garden soil, and keep heat from the sun longer. Water when the soil is dry, which may be daily in hot weather. Always use a thin layer of mulch on top of raised beds around the base of plants, to help them retain moisture better. As for fertilizer, a balanced 10-10-10 fertilizer should be good for most plants in raised beds. Apply lightly in the spring and once a month for the first three months of the growing season, if desired.

What to Plant in your Patio Garden

You really can grow anything you care to grow in a raised bed, even trees and shrubs if you desire. They are most commonly used for vegetables and fruits, herbs, and flowers, for various purposes. A raised bed planter on your patio that is full of colorful flowers and accent plants is certainly a delight, especially if you use your patio for relaxing, entertaining and recreation.

Consider the uses and attributes of your patio when planning raised bed gardening on it. If it is a small patio just outside your kitchen, mostly used for grilling, a kitchen vegetable garden might be perfect. If you have a small balcony or upper-level deck used for sunning or reading, a small herb garden can serve multiple purposes; to spice up cooking, to add herb fragrances to the air, and to serve as an ornament, perhaps in an attractive round or corner bed. Raised beds of trees or shrubs should be saved for ground-level patios, as they benefit from deeper rooting. However, take precautions to limit the direction of the rooting, as you wouldn't want tree roots to upturn your patio stones when they grow older.

Whatever you plant, be sure to check the sun requirements and consider that in your choice and placement of the plants, or of the beds. You can determine how much sun your patio gets by observing it over the course of a few sunny days;

between 6 and 8 hours of direct sunlight is considered a full sun location, while less than that is partial sun. Some patios, if you have a pergola or roof, may be fully shaded areas, in which case you will need to select very shade-tolerant plants, or consider altering your patio so that more sunlight reaches your garden.

Vertical Gardening on the Patio

The most common reason gardeners try out vertical gardening is to make the best use of a small or limited space. You can combine vertical trellising with container gardening on a patio to grow great plants in a tiny amount of space.

Using upwards space rather than outward space is particularly important for vining plants or very fast-spreading plants in small areas, since they can otherwise quickly take over a small container or spread across your patio. Vertical gardening also provides convenience to many gardeners.

There's less bending and weeding, and tasks like pruning, watering, harvesting, and checking for bugs are easier when the plant is growing vertically. Another benefit is that air circulation and sunlight reach the plant more evenly. Most of all, you get much larger yields of vegetable or fruits when these plants are grown vertically. Be aware, though, that these characteristics bring with them other possible issues unlike backyard gardening. Vertical gardens need more frequent watering and fertilizing to keep up with the air and sun.

Vertical Garden Setup

When you are planning your vertical patio garden, think about what plants should go where, You can maximize room on a small patio even further by adding hanging baskets or upside-down style planters hanging from eaves, railings, arbors or canopies. You also can have a few levels of vertical gardens, such as a tall row and a short row of plants.

However, if you place the tall plants in a location that will block the sunlight from reaching the other plants, you must choose a shade-tolerant plant to accompany it, or else adjust your patio garden layout accordingly. Observe the movement of the sun across your patio so you know how much sun your plants will get, and be sure you choose plants that prefer that amount of light.

Most vertical gardens, and certainly all patio gardens, will rely on structures and containers. You have the chance to design the look of your patio to your liking using vertical gardening: you can use arches, arbors, trellises, pyramid-style pole arrangements, planters, wire cages, and even fencing.

Grow Fresh Food or Small Kitchen Garden

Since your patio is often used for outdoor dining anyway, it only seems natural to design a small kitchen garden there. This type of garden can be used to provide your kitchen with fresh herbs, tomatoes, and a sprinkling of other vegetables and fruits throughout the growing season. You will cut down on your grocery expenses while enjoying the fresh flavor of homegrown produce.

A well-planned patio garden can provide you with a variety of herbs, vegetables, or fruits despite the fact that you only have a small space to use. One of the benefits of having only a small area to grow in is the fact that you never become overwhelmed as you can when planting in a large plot. Grow just what you need of each type of herb, vegetable, or fruit to sustain your kitchen. Add in a few flowers to attract beneficial insects and provide extra color to the area.

You do not need to worry over the fact that you are relying on containers for some or all of your patio gardening either. Container growing offers the advantages of being able to move your plants around for more or less sun as well as being able to provide extra drainage if needed. In fact, container gardening is often more controlled than plot gardening so you have an easier time of providing pest and disease control.

No matter what the reason is behind your decision to create a patio garden of your own, once you get started, you are sure to discover many more benefits. Get started today and bring your indoors outdoors for a fine taste of sunshine and freshly-grown produce.

Patio gardens might be your sole garden if you have limited space or lack a yard, but that doesn't mean you have to forgo a beautiful garden of flowers or vegetables. Usually, patio gardens mean growing plants in containers. There are a few differences between backyard gardening and container gardening, but following these general tips will help you grow anything you want in containers on your patio. Soil, sun and water are still the main concern, as with any garden. Place most container plants in a sunny location, unless they are specifically shade-tolerant plants.

Be sure they are potted or planted in loose, rich soil. Regular garden soil is too dense and heavy for potting; it should be loosened and lightened with mulch, peat moss or vermiculite when used in container planting. The containers you choose need to have good drainage, so that water doesn't get trapped around the plant roots. Fit the container to the expected size of the plant, and expect to water and fertilize more often than in a traditional garden. This is because the water will not only run out the bottom of the containers faster but also evaporate faster, taking fertilizer with it.

Watering a Patio Garden

You will need to plan your patio garden with attention to nearby water sources. Is there an outdoor spigot or hose handy, or will you need to carry water from inside the house? Have a plan ready for watering, especially if you are planning to grow a fairly large patio garden. Since soil in containers dries out more quickly than it would in a regular garden, plan on watering daily in hot weather, and every few days in cooler weather. If you're not sure, test the soil with a finger. If it doesn't cling to your finger, you should water.

Since patio gardens require more water than a traditional garden, you may want to consider using water-conserving measures to keep your water usage down. One popular way to do this is to create a rain barrel in your yard or garden. Attaching a downspout to your roof gutter system that directs rainwater into the barrel will help you make the best use of rainfall. Be sure any rain barrel you use has a filter that water must pass through before reaching your garden, to keep out foreign objects, unwanted chemicals and dirt or debris.

Another option is to collect "gray" water from your household. This is water that ordinarily gets wasted through normal household processes, or is slightly used but not dirty. For instance, the first few gallons of water that comes out of the shower or bath faucet before the water temperature warms up often just go down the drain. Collecting the colder water in a multi-gallon bucket and using that on your container plants or patio garden is more than likely all the water you need to use on your garden that day. If time is a concern, you can try self-watering containers, or for larger planters, irrigation systems like soaker or drip hoses can be a blessing.

Patio Garden Pests

While pests and insects may not have the same access to your plants on a patio as they would in a garden, that doesn't mean you can let down your guard completely. They will still be found in patio gardens. Check plants regularly for bugs and signs of disease. Another benefit of patio gardening is that it's easier to check for pests and insects, as the plants are easily movable in their containers, and are more often at eye level. If you do find any pests, separate the plant from the rest of your patio garden, so it can't spread to other plants, and pick or wash bugs off as soon as you can.

Avoid mildew and many other diseases and pests by being careful not to water the foliage of the plants, only the soil, and ensuring your containers are well-drained. The one drawback you may find with having plants on your patio is that you may attract birds, bees and other pollinators to your back door. If you want to keep these off your patio, try to avoid choosing plants that are very attractive to insects and birds, such as berries, brightly colored flowers, and plants that produce nectar.

Patio Garden Options

Patio gardens have several benefits to gardeners, even those who have the room to grow a traditional garden. If your backyard soil is poor, rocky, or overrun with nematodes, moles or other pests, a patio garden offers a new start with fresh soil. Another option is to use patio gardening as a cosmetic addition to your home landscaping. For instance, you could create a trellis covered in plants on your patio to screen an unattractive air conditioning unit on the side of your house. Or, place several tall containers of plants on your patio surrounding or concealing ugly patio features like broken stones, discolored bricks, or columns, fences and railings that seem out of place aesthetically.

The great versatility of container gardening on your patio is that you can have the containers be whatever you like, to match your home, patio, furniture or landscaping style. Wooden barrels, bushel or wire mesh baskets lined with moss, Mediterranean clay pots, inexpensive colorful plastic planters, or sleek modern metal bins all can house successful patio garden elements. Just make sure whatever you choose provides good drainage, with holes in the bottom and a layer of a loose draining medium like pebbles or gravel in the bottom of the container.

Benefits of Patio Gardening

Patio is a paved area outside a home that is usually adjoined and utilized as a recreational spot.

In the past, homeowners didn't pay attention to patio. Many of them thought that their patio space was not a significant part of their homes.

Nonetheless, nowadays many homeowners give great importance to their patio area. There are many advantages that a patio can offer a homeowner, all of which contribute both to the quality of the home as well as the quality of life. Their benefits go far beyond making a home look great. Here are four advantages of a patio.

- ***An excellent place to unwind***

It might be an old saying, but our houses are our castles. It is where we all go to relax at the end of a hard day of work day. One common advantage of having a patio is that it is a place to unwind; allowing one to enjoy the fresh air without being drenched by the rain or hit by the sun. We know that every person has their own ways of unwinding, but a patio prove to be great place to relax and just forget all your worries. Adding a fireplace to the patio can spruce up its look, making it a distinctive place to sit and unwind.

- ***It is an all season outdoor***

Sometimes the weather can be unpredictable. It will be a pity to allow a sudden rainstorm or heat wave to prevent you from relaxing in your yard over the weekend. You can enjoy the warmth of the summer, from shade and comfort, hence avoiding the problems related with prolonged exposure to the sun like heat exhaustion, sunburn, or heat stroke in some cases. This can be achieved through patio blinds. Additionally, rain presents no havoc to a well installed patio and one can enjoy the sound of the rains on his roof whilst outdoors.

- ***It is an entertainment area***

Another added advantage of installing a patio to your home is that it offers an excellent place to entertain particularly for homeowners who have smaller houses. Whether you are planning a barbecue, a get-together with family or friends, or relaxing with your mate and a couple of bottles of beer, patio provides a great outdoor area in which to do all these. You can bet that entertainment factor of patio is among the defining reasons as to why most people consider having them installed.

- ***Adds value to a home***

Along with the advantages of entertainment area give rise to value for your home. Depending upon the present value of your home, adding a patio can considerably boost the valuation of your property. Often times, when people want to purchase or lease a home, the exclusion or inclusion of an entertainment area can either make or break the sale.

Patios offer many benefits, which is why you ought to give it a thought. These are the advantages you can get by adding patio to your existing house, or adding it to the plans of the house you intend to construct.

Downside of Patio Gardening

Those who are confined to city living do not always have access to a yard wherein they can plant a garden. Therefore, a patio garden becomes their next best option in order to be able to enjoy freshly picked vegetables and herbs during the summer months. However, as good as a patio garden may be, there are some disadvantages of having one.

- *Limited Amount Of Space*

One of the biggest problems with having a patio garden is the fact that there really is not too much room in most cases. The patio is designed for a small patio table and chairs and a barbecue, and not much else. Therefore, space is generally limited, especially when growing larger vegetables such as cucumbers, tomatoes, peppers and zucchini. As a result, a patio garden might not always be suitable for growing the bigger vegetables.

• **_Requires Numerous Pots_**

Another disadvantage of having a patio garden is that you need a number of pots. First you need small containers in which to start the seeds, and then a lot of plants need to be transplanted into a larger pot. It might not seem like a lot of pots at first, but then, when the summer is over, you now have to find a place to store them. This can be difficult, especially if you live in a small apartment where space is limited.

• **_Needs Frequent Watering_**

Plants that are grown within a pot also require frequent watering. This is because the root systems are contained within a pot, and do not have access to a constant supply of water. Therefore they need to be watered more frequently than anything that is allowed to grow freely in the garden, especially on hot summer days.

- ## *Not Enough Sun*

Depending on which side of the house the patio is located, the plants might not get enough sunlight to prosper and yield a good crop. A south-facing patio is best, as it will receive the maximum amount of sunlight, but other patios might not be able to provide enough natural light. Another thing to consider is that the plants are located closer to the building, which also takes away from the sunlight.

Despite the disadvantage of a patio garden, there are also benefits that can make the time and efforts pay off quite well. Those include fresh produce that does not contain any pesticides. Also, you will have access to the produce when you need it.

Ways to Be a Great Gardener

Every Gardener knows how important it is to take time to reflect on ways in which you can improve the performance. Gardeners are observant people and as such, they can scrutinize, monitor, and take different signals from the plants so as to make a determination on whether the plants are the way they need to be.

Most professional gardeners make use of approaches that are idiosyncratic, so as to give the gardens everything they need. There are many tips that can help you be the best gardener and they include:

Design

Form and texture are more important than the color. The atmosphere and space are also very important. If you notice that the shrubs have no space below, you may need some pruning. You need to think about the design of your space and decide on what you should plant there and in what quantities.

Sowing

This is a very important part of growing a garden. When you sow your seeds, you need to water them using some warm water. Avoid using the ice-cold water as it ends up delaying the germination. After they germinate, it is important that you only handle the seedlings using the leaves since they are tougher than stems at this point.

Planting

When you are planting, then you need to think about every aspect of the process so as not to affect your plants negatively. Make sure you plant in the correct soil combination.

If you have the funds for it, then a greenhouse is definitely an amazing idea and definitely worth a try. Even a greenhouse that is not heated extends your season for growing your own good and increasing the summers. A greenhouse can be an invaluable addition to the garden as it can help you extend the range in the most incredible ways.

For real gardeners, it is important to listen to your own mood and do what you think should be done to improve the garden. You should choose the ideal time to move the plants as long as there is enough soil, shade, and a water source. This is what allows the plants to establish even more quickly.

It is important to act early. For example, if you feel young tree is not located in the ideal point, and then you need to move it early. Do not wait until such a tree has already matured so as to start thinking of ways to deal with it.

Vegetables

If you chose to grow your vegetables in pots, it is important to have a shade so as to slow down the bolting. You can use mulch to stop weeds from invading the vegetable area and this works well too. You need to consider which vegetables grow together. Doing this helps you make the most of the gardening experience by easing processes like pollination and so on.

Pests

Understanding pests is also a part of good gardening. There are some pests that will play dead if they are disturbed. It is important to stay alert and notice any changes in your plants. A good gardener always finds a way to deal with pest and diseases at all times so as to improve yield.

Plant Suggestions

 Almost any herb can be grown in a container. The following vegetables are easy, productive choices for container gardening:

Asian Greens

Such as Bok Choy. Use a container that is at least 20 inches deep by 12 inches wide per plant.

Beans

Need a pot that is minimum 12 inches deep / 5-gallon capacity, and a strong trellis structure for support. A larger pot would allow additional plants like kale and celery to grow alongside. There are bush varieties that don't require support.

Beets

Direct seed into a 2 to 5-gallon container.

Carrots

Container size (6 – 15 inches deep) may vary according to the carrot type you're growing and planting depth it requires. It's best to grow the shorter varieties such as Thumbelina or Short 'N Sweet. Direct seed into a 2 to 5-gallon container. Thin carrot seedlings (when they're 2 inches tall) to about 2 – 3 inches apart.

Cucumber

2 transplants per 5-gallon container. There are bush varieties that don't require support.

Edible Flowers

Besides being edible and useful in dishes from soups to sauces, stir fry, salads, teas and even ice cream, these flowers can be used to brighten arrangements – marigolds, calendula, viola, nasturtium, rose petals, hibiscus, citrus blossoms and many of the blossoms of herbs typically grown.

Eggplant

One eggplant per 5-gallon container, at least 12 inches deep for each plant.

Garlic

Choose a pot that is at least 6-8 inches deep and as wide as possible; you'll need to leave 5-6 inches of space between each clove you plant.

Kale

Can be grown in small sized pots. Each plant requires at least 6 inches of space.

Kohlrabi

3 transplants per 5-gallon container.

Lettuce

One transplant per 1-gallon container. Choose a wide planter rather than deep; six inches deep is fine. When planting, make sure to leave at least four inches between each plant. Leaf lettuces can be grown more closely than head lettuces. You can harvest leaf lettuce multiple times throughout the (cool) growing season.

Okra

Dwarf okra varieties are more suitable for containers. Pot should be at least 3 gallons in size. Ideally, a 5-gallon pot that is 10-12 inches deep and similar in diameter would be better. Best to choose a black colored pot as okra loves heat.

Onion

In 1 gallon or larger container, thin to 2 inches between green onions and 6 inches between bulb onions.

Peas

Direct seed into a 5-gallon container and thin to 5 inches apart. Choose a dwarf or bush type variety and do regular and frequent watering as peas prefer slightly moist soil. Peppers and chilies – A large pot that is at least 12 inches deep and 16 inches across is optimum, or a 5-gallon container. It may require a cage or stick for support.

Radish

In 2 gallon or larger container, thin to 3 inches apart. Can also grow them in small and wide pots. A planter that is just 6 inches deep is enough but if you want to grow larger varieties use an 8 to 10-inch-deep pot. Allow 3 inches of space between each plant.

Spinach

In 1 gallon or larger container, at least 6-8 inches deep, space 3 inches apart.

Strawberries

Minimum pot 10-12 inches in diameter by 8 inches deep. Cultivars adapted to Florida include Camarosa (best for north FL home gardeners), Sweet Charlie, Florida Belle, Florida 90, and Festival. June bearing.

Summer squash

Summer squashes (Zucchini) are more productive than winter squashes. Plant two transplants per 5-gallon container. There are bush varieties that don't require support.

Swiss chard

4 plants per 5-gallon container. Each plant requires at least 6 inches of space.

Tomatoes

One transplant per 5-gallon container, at least 20 inches across for standard and vining types. The easiest to grow in containers are dwarf varieties of the determinate (reach a certain size and stop growing) type. Bushsteak, Bush Champion, Early Girl Bush, and Window Box Roma are just a few of the many choices. They need little to no support. Also grow cherry tomatoes as they are very high yielding with long staying power.

Additional Plants made for Patio Life:

'Baby Cakes' blackberry, 'Mini Love' watermelon, 'Raspberry Shortcake' raspberry, 'Angel Red' pomegranate, 'Little Ragu' sweet bay, 'Celestial' fig, Meyer lemon, dwarf navel orange, Key lime, Kaffir lime, limequat, 'Truly Tiny' banana, 'Smooth Cayenne' pineapple, turmeric, and culinary ginger.